Turnagain Ptarmigan!

Where Did You Go?

James Guenther

Illustrated by Shannon Cartwright

PAWS IV

PUBLISHED BY SASQUATCH BOOKS

James Guenther is a teacher in Ketchikan, Alaska, where he lives with his wife and their four children. This is his first book.

Shannon Cartwright has been illustrating PAWS IV children's books for more than twenty years. She and her husband live in Alaska's Talkeetna Mountains, near Denali.

Printed in Hong Kong.
Distributed in Canada by Raincoast Books, Ltd.

05 04 03 02 00   5 4 3 2 1

Library of Congress Cataloging in Publication Data
Guenther, James.
         Turnagain ptarmigan! Where did you go? / written by James Guenther; illustrated by Shannon Cartwright.
                  p.   cm.
         Summary: A child watches as a ptarmigan changes its appearance and actions as the seasons change.
         ISBN 1-57061-237-4 (alk. paper)
         ISBN 1-57061-271-4 (hardcover)
         [1. Ptarmigans—Fiction. 2. Stories in rhyme.] I. Title: Turnagain, Ptarmigan. II. Cartwright, Shannon, ill.
         III. Title.
         PZ8.3.G946 Tu 2000
         [E]—dc21   00-036570

SASQUATCH BOOKS / 615 Second Avenue, Suite 260 / Seattle, WA 98104
800-775-0817 / www.SasquatchBooks.com / books@SasquatchBooks.com

This book is dedicated to the curiosity of children everywhere . . .
and to the teachers who strive to nurture it.
—J. G.

To the wonders of the high country, its inhabitants, and most of all, to Keith and Vee.
—S. C.

Thank you to wildlife photographer Tom Walker, wildlife artist David Totten,
Jim Rothenbuhler at the Knotty Shop, and Dan Gibson, ornithologist at
the University of Alaska Museum in Fairbanks.

Turnagain ptarmigan!
Where did you go?

Look very carefully.
I'm here in the snow.

Turnagain ptarmigan!
Don't be so shy.

I'm dancing with Wind,
Up here in the sky.

Turnagain ptarmigan!
Asleep in the snow?

I burrow down deep
When the Northern Lights glow.

Turnagain ptarmigan!
Springtime is here!

Then I'll dapple my feathers
As the snows disappear.

Turnagain ptarmigan!
What's happening today?

Strutting and tail-fanning!
It's a courtship display.

Turnagain ptarmigan!
Where could you be?

I'm dressed up for summer
And under a tree.

Turnagain ptarmigan!
Come out and play!

I must stay on my nest
With the eggs that I lay.

Turnagain ptarmigan!
I hear young ones peeping.

They're always exploring.
We wish they were sleeping!

Turnagain ptarmigan!
Are you having a meeting?

These berries are sweet.
We're over here eating.

Turnagain ptarmigan!
Where are you, my friend?

With the soft snow falling,
I'm changing again.

Turnagain ptarmigan!
Are you here all alone?

I'm here with ten friends.
Do you need to be shown?

Little child, little child!
I've come searching for you!

You silly white bird!
I can play that game too!

Can you?

Fall feather

Blueberry

Low-bush cranberry

Winter plumage

Cloudberry

Winter tracks

Crowberry

Willow

The Willow Ptarmigan
The Alaska State Bird

The willow ptarmigan lives throughout most of Alaska and northern Canada, as well as in the high latitudes of Europe and Asia. A master of camouflage, the ptarmigan (the "p" is silent) changes its plumage from season to season to blend in with its surroundings. In the winter, the ptarmigan is white like the snow, except for its black tail. As the seasons change, its plumage molts almost continually, transforming into patterns of gold, red, brown, and black. In the fall, it starts turning white again for the coming of winter.

Willow ptarmigan prefer high alpine valleys, arctic tundra, willow scrub, and muskeg. They often spend time in stands of dwarf willow, eating the twigs and buds. They also eat seeds, leaves, berries, flowers, catkins (seed husks), and bugs. Their close relatives are the rock ptarmigan and the white-tailed ptarmigan.

In the winter, the ptarmigan's feet are like little snowshoes, covered with short feathers that make it easy to walk on top of the snow. In fact, the ptarmigan's Latin name, *Lagopus*, means "rabbit foot," and their feet certainly resemble those of a snowshoe hare! To escape predators or find shelter, ptarmigan will dive straight into snow banks, breaking through the crust with their sturdy breasts.

When spring arrives, mating ptarmigan use their sharp claws to scratch depressions into the ground. Working together, the mating pair line the depression with feathers, grasses, and tundra, creating a simple but well-hidden nest. The female lays from five to twelve eggs. The eggs are covered with red spots that turn black when the eggs are exposed to the air, giving them a mottled appearance.

The male willow ptarmigan is a dedicated father. He is the only one in the grouse family who will guard the female while she is nesting and help her raise the chicks. He will even fly down and crash into a predator to distract it from the nest. If something happens to the female, the male will take over the care of the chicks.

Both the male and the female ptarmigan have a red comb over their eyes, although it's hidden under their feathers most of the winter. The male's comb is more pronounced, especially during the mating season. The ptarmigan's calls range from growls to cackles to croaks. During courtship, the male cries loudly, *go-back, go-back, go-backa, go-backa, go-backa.*

In 1958, Alaskan school children elected the willow ptarmigan to be the official Alaska state bird.

Spring plumage   Summer plumage   Fall plumage   Winter plumage

Female   Male   Female   Male